*Point of Sale*

Also by Peter Sansom from Carcanet

*Everything You've Heard is True*
*January*

PETER SANSOM

# *Point of Sale*

CARCANET

First published in Great Britain in 2000 by
Carcanet Press Limited
4th Floor, Conavon Court
12–16 Blackfriars Street
Manchester M3 5BQ

A CIP catalogue record for this book
is available from the British Library

ISBN 1 85754 484 6

The publisher acknowledges financial assistance
from the Arts Council of England

Set in Monotype Garamond by XL Publishing Services, Tiverton
Printed and bound in England by SRP Ltd, Exeter

# Contents

# Acknowledgements

*Atlanta Review*, *Brando's Hat*, *The Guardian*, *PN Review*, *Poetry Ireland Review*, *www.centrifugalforces.co.uk*; *Hello New* (edited by John Agard, Orchard Books); *Last Words* (edited by Don Paterson and Jo Shapcott, Picador) and *An Enduring Flame* and *Poetry in the Parks* (edited by Wendy Bardsley, Smith Settle and Sigma Books). Five of the poems are the result of commissions: I'm grateful to the Salisbury Festival; Winchester Festival; *The Mail on Sunday*; *The Observer* and the *Times Educational Supplement*.

Eleven of these poems appeared in the pamphlet *Talk Sense* (Slow Dancer): I'd like to thank John Harvey for his continuing encouragement. The fruit poems are responses to drawings by Ted Schofield and are dedicated to him. Andrew Wilson helped me keep faith in some of the poems here. Warm thanks also to my friends at Marks and Spencer and the Poetry Society (the Poetry Places scheme, through the Arts Council Lottery Fund). And not least to Naomi Jaffa and Michael Laskey of the Aldeburgh Poetry Trust, my love and thanks.

*Driving at Night*


The res through trees
is a lake or calm sea on whose far shore
a holiday is waiting, a fire laid in the grate,
the larder stocked with tins, milk in the fridge,
and on the hearth a vase of new tulips.
There's a table at a window and cabin seats
like a ship against wood walls that make the room
small, snug. An oil lamp completes the effect
of a time before cars, and merges our shadows.
Snow meets and holds to the pane
with its jumbled view of a harbour;
fishing boats answer the tide and open throttle.
Upstairs the bed's aired, coverlet turned down.
At which point I dab the brakes for a bend
and the holiday disappears, money
we've not got. The rich piano on the radio
is like driving through music, Haydn that contains
a little of what Mozart would do
and is itself, travelling two centuries.
Pine forest, my favourite, on this stretch
that crowds either side of what's deserted,
so twisting here the many cats eyes are bright
a mile or two from the outskirts of a city.
Our life is a holiday, even the work and preparation,
this car on a minor road, a small house on the coast,
and the music leading itself where it must go
complete in its dark collocation of notes,
each separate phrase that can be understood
by the ear only, the tock now of wipers
across the first clinging flakes of a flurry.

## Sit-com

The baby is at an age to say Oh fuck,
The middle one sleeps off E with her boyfriend
and has her prints taken shoplifting.
The eldest has his arse in the sofa
and trails a guitar lead even to the loo;
Oasis make him sneer at exams.
The gas electric mortgage council tax road tax
and catalogue in the same week is a joke,
not to mention the phone, tied up 24 hours
with trauma to step over on the stairs.
The cats bring fleas and a coating of fur.
The job is running to stand still and everyone
else in a company car or sleeping rough.
Your dad died convinced you were his dad.
Mum is trapped by her legs in a flat
you don't visit enough. And your friends
your friends are a box of bastards you never see.
You love your wife and your wife loves you
but neither of you believe it.

## Some Night, by Chance

Some night, by chance, you'll meet a man
who says your thoughts – a band a book a film,
parents. He'll drink the same drink and smoke your brand,
guess the punchline and still laugh, still
finding it funny because it's yours. You won't kiss
or hold hands, even, for days of meeting
accidentally on purpose. Can you believe this?
His eyes stop your heart. You grin like idiots.

Some night, by chance, you'll meet a man
on the last bus. He asks directions
to some other place, then gets off after you.
There are streetlights linking the short walk home,
but you're nervous, his hollow step a moment yards
behind yours, which quickens, not quick enough
by the blade of dark, the garages
he pushes you towards. Is this more likely?

Or some night, by chance, you'll meet a man
in Sainsbury's say. He's married or living-with,
you can see that from the trolley and yet
there's something there when you catch his eye
on cereals, sauces, the jam aisle.
You pay at adjacent checkouts. Go
as if agreed into the café, the only free table.
And he is both those other men. Believe me.

## Song

Come home, if you can.
You don't need to explain
anything to anyone.
Come home alive
and not as some
would have us believe.
The security light will light
your way, however late
you make it to our blue back door.
We'll still be up, in any case
even at, particularly at, that hour.
In any case your key will fit the lock.

How young you've got,
when I think of you
there among so much
that's evidently untrue.
A tree, a garden gate, next door's shed.
Come home with that smirk
that practically drove us mad.
Come home with that look
that'll tell us what it's like
wherever it is, whatever it is
you are now, and that
you're not going back.

## Clinical Depression

I drove in my virtuous car
with the dozen years of growing up
for a passenger, and found him,
and sat alongside in the day room

to say I'm here, once a week
for a month. Brother. Half brother.
Cheek bones from dad's side
and the thin mouth, wet eyes.

One day, overcast, we walked
by the res across the road.
Sailing boats need rowing boats
or dinghies; at anchor the breeze

nods their masts. Boys go by
on mountain bikes, and we talk
and go nowhere, back to the block
he suddenly can't believe is right.

He knows I get things wrong
and maybe I've got this wrong
for a reason. He has to see
my car in the car park, go round

to see the key fit the lock
and Mary's things before he'll try
the automatic doors, the corridors,
and still there's a panic

not to be wrong, to read the curious
ward name and know it's home.
This is days before they put the guess
of volts through him, a treatment

he signed himself to because
his sister knew it worked, or might,
and because by then
nobody was there to question it.

Cheaper than drugs, cheaper than talk,
that's just politics. What the rest
would expect. This is the real world,
and his wife, whatever you say,

however you say it, will stay dead,
every morning, every night,
and all the time there is,
so many months after, inbetween.

## Canal. Midnight,

give or take. Overcast but
light enough to see the curve of water
trapped between one place and another.
Cars, one or two, fast along the valley tops.
Warm windows let into the steep opposite
and behind them tellys keep people from
one last cup before they turn in.
And here is the towpath.
My eyes are accustomed
and by the lockgates I scuffle my trainers
in couch grass for the weights hidden there
that once were snug and unused
on their stand in the spare room.
I pull out the cord and fasten them,
a reef knot taking me to Mrs Morgan's class,
and then I walk like a cowboy or a martian
in this strange gravity
to the shallow edge among the reeds
and lumber in, icy, up to the knees,
the waist, the chest. The water resists
but crumples as I wade out of my depth,
who never learned to swim.
That was everything
until, some hours later,
I clamber beneath the blink of an angler
out into next morning,
undo what held me under,
and strike out across a field,
my back to where I was,
my pockets empty but dry as tinder,
to where I will be, all of us, a family.

*Nocturne*

Night, early morning, on a coach.
I'm forgotten in favour
of the novel I'm dreaming, reading, dreaming,

the landscape a dot-to-dot of houselights,
bordered by sodium, a motorway
that will cross our path with moving lives.

After one day in a place with tables
and clothes just this side of suits,
paper cups of coffee, I'm going home.

Behind sleeping windows
expressions – bland? theatrical? –
rehearse another, longer night.

The word eternal comes to me
but I can no more use it than be it –
that's Yorkshire out there.

The beautiful girl on the seat in front
is my daughter, step daughter I should say,
snoring to wake the dead;

and though the forest comes down
out of its enclosure
to follow us, like a living thing,

it stops where the meat warehouses start,
the ring road; the far hills
are slag heaps, what's the word, reclaimed

and the dead wake bolt upright
in my book with a book in their hands,
minutes now from the bus station.

## Summer Evening
### after Stanley Cook

Every summer comes an opaque evening
before the beach is photos and the leaves
let go to relight autumn. It's brisk in Wickes
and the garden centre's scented colours
are loaded in the backs of estates. In parks
that saw offices undress for lunch
lads career in the wake of the World Cup
and wood after deliberate wood finds
a path in its own curve to the jack.
Everywhere is couples, and pushchairs
that make sense of last year or last but one,
till pubs overflow round continental tables
on main roads, laughing like it might last.

Sooner or later, swans on a river
disprove the moon they paddle through,
cameoed by willows. The rowing boat
moored there is a temptation you decline,
though all the time you walk, taking
the long cut to the car park, you imagine
being out on that water, the drag
and viscous ripples as you pull,
then shipping oars and just letting it drift.

# Point of Sale

ADVERTISEMENT

This is a verse diary of my time as Poetry Society writer in residence
to Marks and Spencer. From it the reader may gather something about
workshops and a good deal about rail travel; still more about how a
little media attention may turn a person's head: but precious little
about M&S. I am sorry about this. There are two borrowings to own
up to, both in the Norwich poem: Byron's lines about making people
think, and Keats's observation – often in my mind while I wrote these
pieces – that 'everything is worth, as tradesmen say, what it will fetch'.

## FIRST DAY

My bag not holding a bomb, it's ticketed
with St Michael, and I queue for a pass
among expense accounts, chic that fits in
in London, or this part. I'm from the sticks
and the receptionist's never heard of me.

The marble foyer is stately home
but a swirl of steps leads one century
to the next, and the smoking room
when I get there's a meritocracy
of horses for courses, sweatshirt and Armani.

A black lad in a white coat and grocery trilby
wheels a trolley of bananas to the canteen
called Restaurant. A woman like a model
who is a model, exact size ten for a living,
is the focus of a camera only she sees,

continually. Then I'm kidgloved down corridors
of rooms big-windowed like a zoo
to meet IT, this designer, that, a cube
of dummies and needle-and-thread, the sharp-end
of CAD: this neck of the wood's

like a liberal college, all colour and coffee-cups.
Next an airlock you need a smartcard for
against industrial espionage. It seems
to be labels for soup tins. Further,
Furniture and not knowing where to look

through Lingerie, the pull-out bookstacks
of wardrobe racks. More smiles. Finally
shake hands with Press and on the way back
in a crossroads of plush and softlighting
a director with the air of a man

in a light-up bow-tie or polkadot at least.
Not typical, Julia says, but then
none of them are. As an afterthought
pop in here, a room of front-loaders
putting jumpers in eight hours

through five years of hot cycles. What it is
to be lambswool, shrunk hardly at all
at the end of the day but bobbled enough
to call the entire line back
from Paris, Hong Kong, Dublin, Strasbourg,

Huddersfield.


MANCHESTER AIRPORT FOR BELFAST

From here you can go anywhere, though mine's
a domestic flight, depending on your point of view –
a joke to us, 'don't get blown to bits' and how
Christmas pudding shows up like semtex.
It's the February before the ceasefire
and I'm starry-eyed for the third time in my life
about the commonplace miracle
of a heap of metal leaving the ground.

\*

Ferried in by PR – really a person
underneath – in a two-seater sports, I'm met
by a microphone, the local angle
on what a poet does (or is doing)
among the knitwear; then TV
('did you bring a change of clothes?') –
some cutaways in Lingerie
with half a dozen pressganged smiling staff,
before the reason I'm here: thirty people
in a room surprising their real selves
into life in language, what words do to you
when you can't not let them.

28 women, the manager,
and a lad damaged in some way. Everyone:
the task times the pressure of the group
getting it airborne; patterns of sound and idea
keeping it up there, the process
that for a while is the only place to be.
They read back to themselves,
the commonplace miracle of people
saying who they are to people listening.

\*

After, I'm a prat, an underwater lunch
with the headsumps, a finger-buffet with me
all thumbs and foot in mouth.
I've learned some shop floor lingo
about ambient food and fallow spaces
but it stays words on the page to camera,
a trail for *Poetry in Store, Tonight 6.30* –
when the poetry is them, already back
on the tills and loose produce, what the
possibly tongue-in-cheek bra-fitter
called her 'work identity'.

i

This floor's a sumptuous hotel
of corridors, rich walls of discreet art.
A dainty uniform and dainty trolley
wheeling from the Directors' Kitchen

the story of a scheme where everyone here
tries another life twice a year,
and the director who refused because the rules
meant she had to catch a bus.

So many surprises, this place,
like funding off-the-wall not just
off-the-peg designers and keeping
that sort of sponsorship under their hat,

putting something back. It makes sense
they have their own health centre
and screen routinely for breast cancer,
as well as refining the Howard Hughes super

structure that kept Jane Mansfield afloat.
I picture that
and the hamster wheel of a running belt
where upstairs they're jogging to *Wham!*;

and look down on an open-top tour
stopped in traffic, a leafleteer in Equity
resting under a deerstalker. Look up again,
Canary Wharf, the Telecom Tower, sky

blue as a Caneletto, only dearer.

ii

The staff restaurant. An electric
bulletin board runs above chilled water
its repetoire of shares down (8.5 at 1pm)
and ex-Littlewoods new store opening at. A tray

and the wig you notice second that says
'OK, so I've been ill', the tables, the chairs.
And there's my brother on the other hand
who'd walk miles – this clicks into place –

because he couldn't manage the coins and asking
of getting the C7 to Huthwaite.
It's easy to sneer, wherever that director
is up there, wealthier in the one day

she wouldn't give up of her car and driver
than he is in a year. He mended roads
for a living. And I remember that line,
'all my friends are unemployable',

written by a friend of mine, a poet working
killing hours in a plastic-mouldings factory.


POETRY SOCIETY: INDUCTION DAY

A ghost of myself, like most meetings
I fade in and out among the guy
with the Russian hat and shades
in March indoors; black, who wonders
how aware we are of diversity
and rather than wait for an answer
talks for three quarters of an hour
of look at me. I don't catch his name.
And Sarah who wants to know
about the conceptual in my work.
We help ourselves to shortbread
and a glass of water. John and Sarah
uncover the political in their art:
*for botanical read colonial.*
Sarah has a Russian tank
commander's watch; it loses a minute
every hour. John's is a fob-watch,
no dearer than having time
strapped to your wrist. His life
seems to be a poem; Sarah's
a garden she puts her back into.

Not quite for a joke I set off
the fire alarm of my enthusiasm,
which is part of the job too
especially in meetings. But really
I could almost walk through the wall. Neither
John nor Sarah drive. I'm thinking
about the new car tomorrow,
a Volvo paid for by the lottery
that brought me here, and about
the people who will write
because I ask them to
that either friends or nobody will read.

*

There's a snort when I don't want to read
what the press says. It goes without saying
I'm self-obsessed in this shrine
to self-obsession, but I just like
the attention. They can say what they like.
My watch is cheap, and slightly fast,
a rough idea for always running late.
It's not the snort but what it says
when I don't snap back, but have to here,
sky-writing haikus, poems in flowerbeds,
such good ideas, such easy targets,
when we all mean well, if not the best,
ignorant as we must be what that is;
poetry as public art or installation,
or as vocation; hold in your head
the poem entire and it's part of you
and you part of it. If you say so,
though nobody does.

Leicester De Montfort, from a train.
I saw Soft Machine there. 75.
Some of their tunes were fuck all
over and over, and shit hot.
The summer before I cut my hair,
too young for hippy, too old for punk
and grew a beard to suit
the desert boots and duffle coat.
It sounded better, I guess,
if you smoked the stuff that wrote it,
but they were fogeys really,
and I needed to stay alert.
A lot of notes round simple
chord progressions, profligate
because they could. A drummer
like five hands and John Etheridge,
a guitar you never knew where
he'd go or how, but it was
the keyboards that made it. Cross-legged
in quadrophonic, kaftans were OK
though only just and people
still slept on people's floors
like they do or woke in strange beds
to introduce themselves. Patchouli,
cheesecloth, *The Brothers Karamazov*,
*Siddhartha*, and Kevin Ayers
who started with the Softs before
*Whatever She Brings We Sing*;
but round the corner of that one
endless summer there was Talking Heads
about to hit me like a train,
*they say patience is a virtue*
*but I don't have much time.*

Too late for the train, I drive with Melvyn Bragg,
the A1 to Darlington, which turns
from a dark and crowded placename
picked up somewhere to a sunny stroll
through a market town on market day.

\*

Before the store, a session with a group
that's met ten years of Monday mornings
to share unpublished fiction, unplayed plays,
poems that rhyme and sentimentalize.
I know these strangers. The twenty-something lad
into performance and shock; the thirty-odd
sci-fi guy; the woman with pen-and ink
booklets of written-up holidays:
she hands me New England; the two retired
jacks-of-all-trades, ringbound A4 longhand;
the guidelines from Mills and Boon;
articles in the *Echo*, verse on Cleveland Radio.

They know me too. The tutor
anxious not to condescend, easy to impress,
who mustn't think too big for his boots
and searches for change for the tea.
I taught them ten years, an evening class
and saw them one-off up and down the country.
So I know if I knew them several would be friends,
one or two brighter, more gifted, later
better-known or wiser than to care.
Though they never write in class,
they write for me, for themselves, and are
what they always are, a community ...

\*

The group leader's part-time at the store
and leads me there, ten to the dozen
with local history, and the Barbara Taylor Bradford
they filmed here. She's writing one herself
or Catherine Cookson. Every third person

says hello, from church, from swimming,
a charity, the former mayor
smiling past his mobile, not breaking stride.
Her project is getting everyone in print,
if need be funding it themselves, not those
faceless wankers (surely I've misheard)
in that conglomerate of publishing.
We pause and I look at her again.
It's only when you look up, she says, you see
what the town's really like, above
the high street stores the same everywhere.
And here we are. They're waiting for us.


## ROMFORD

I'm fat, me, I get called names.
Tall for my age, I get called names.
Poor at our house, I get called names.
We're rich, my family, I get called names.
Asian me, I get called names.
Good in class, I get called names.
I wear glasses, I get called names.
Bottom of the class, I get called names.
Got red hair, I get called names.
In a wheelchair, I get called names.
Quiet, me, I get called names.
Not from round here, I get called names.
Dad left home, I get called names.
A teacher me, I get called names.
A dinner lady, I get called names.
Deputy Head, I get called names.
Head teacher, I get called names.
I'm hard, me.


## THE BIG BREAKFAST

A train half-empty courtesy
Planet 24 that pulls in at 10.30,
St Pancras; then a black cab
parts the shiny streets, the fairy tale
bridge we cross, the sleepless river.

The Holiday Inn is a hotel. It looks
like luxury you were meant for
and makes me timid, my awkward clothes,
the hand-me-down pushchair
and Mary at home anywhere.

The room's a box. The shower
won't shut off. We might drown
in this scalding farce or bring the ceiling down
till we work it out.
                          Up at four
for the car to the house.

Taped cables and drizzle.
The Green Room is a portakabin, the set
much smaller than you'd think
and just as crowded. Even in run-through
the camera loves Denise. On air

they step up a million volts,
Johnny Vaughan casually
incandescent, what puts him
where he is. I remember the Corrs
and being miked up, and talking,

making up verse, veering
between loving it
and can't-be-arsed, like most things
I do most days, as it happens,
the camera running then as now.


BAKER STREET: 2

Given the freedom of the place,
the run, I should say, I career

slowly the generous stairwells to
B540 Poultry (stet) or

B518, Fish and Frozen Fish.
The Lowry here is a statement

but not the same one as the same one
on the stairs of Hudds Poly library,

and for all I know this next to the Fish
is original. Walk, little stick people, across

from John Prescott pictured at the wheel
of a juggernaut that runs on natural gas

a 25th the air pollution of diesel. This
is Physical Distribution Foods, that

is thin houses, ginnel, streetlights
in the drizzle and washing line midweek

hankering after the freedom of, say,
Bridget Riley, whose colours say

what they like. (Skips of flat cartons
now outside a shuttered office.) Despite

the works' chimney black as Blake's,
Lowry's slinky cat and a girl bowling a hoop

gesture at more including for instance
fun. The one I remember better in Huddersfield,

actually is actually of Huddersfield
(Chapel Hill). The moral of which escapes me.

Shall I say 'place the of freedom the given'
and make as much sense of it, face to crotch

with a cardboard girl in knickers and bra
upside down in a studio window. No,

I call time at Pensions and Health Services
as one ought, seeing none of it, sensible

to the last, and make my way back
to exercise the right to kill myself

with the others in the smoking room.

Each week on the cakewalk
to complimentary coffee, a different scandal
in the hands of the same booked seats –
Gary Glitter, George Michael, the Major with a Cadet;
what men will do for sex and how
we like to read it. I pass gripping thrillers,
half-built arcades, the score of a string quintet
whole I imagine in the man's head.
Mobile phones go without saying. Laptops.
I pause longer than's proper
by a suit explaining why women's suits
are dearer to manufacture. All corporate life
is here, and the first class I guess at,
except the chairman, and the tea girl.
Jeffrey Archer straight-face to camera
batting back what, with such a lovely wife,
he'd want prostitutes for. Or that acid woman,
*You see I don't think sex is dirty,*
for Woody Allen's, *You must be doing it wrong,*
and what as it turned out
Mia Farrow thought to that.

Labouring back against the inertia
of coming into Bedford, there's a fur wrap
in this weather saying *Shopping
and Fucking's just me,* and George Michael,
when he could have anyone, madness,
which was the point, she supposes,
like that Hugh Grant. And the million
daily peccadillos, I suppose
– at a standstill now – that never make
the papers, which make as little sense
as the way we hurt each other
and call it business. People get off
for work, get on. Simplistic to think
of those shareholders in only benefit books
and scratchcards, a lifetime of six numbers
to fund the opera – and now me,
my walk-on part in poetry. Meow:
your working class roots are showing dearie.
Well touch them up, you gorgeous hunk,
nobody's looking

Here instead with a sixth form
in miles of sideways Pennine rain,
on the side of a valley, a millowner's house
that was Ted Hughes's, now is anyone's
for a week of no demands but writing.

Sixteen bodies on the brink
of being who they are, only more so,
that poems, I think or say I think, will discover;
and with their teachers, a woman with that rare talent
for expressing the ego through others
and a man who on the third night adds nitol
to wine to join the living. My age,
whose hopes evade his temperament
and misuse his gifts, witty, eating his heart out
for the kids who love him. And who am I,
Dr Freud, he might ask, my own ambition stalled
and taken to talking to itself...

*

... Negating the self
as a tutor is a sort of megalomania.
I drink merlot with the grown-ups
at the long, candlelit evening table
where tomorrow we'll write in the person
of the left shoe in a shoebox, a hoover,
a stained-glass window in a derelict church.
Asked to suggest mine, a girl
looks me in the eye to say a zip. The room
as one person explodes with laughter.
I see what she means, which is why I begin

Trust me.
I've been in this pair since I was made.
Gold, to look at anyway. The more worn I get
the more he thinks he's a star, bending
to strike a match on me. Prat. Zip I go,
zip up, zip down. I know

you're waiting for when things
get interesting, last thing at night
or caught short. Look at it

from my side. Not much of a life
and no, that's a t-shirt I've got my teeth in.

All you really want's a snigger, isn't it,
the zip fastner, the fly.
I made my inventor a millionaire.
What's velcro to me? Whose hand
is that? A strange hand
brings us, yes,
to the interesting bit
but there are rules. I was told

keep it shut, keep schtum, button it.


CHELTENHAM

The store seems endless with mirrors,
a sort of style. Easy to see
how you could love
the packaging, from patent leather
to foil wrapped crisps, jars of oil
like spirits or jewellery. I ride
the smooth escalator to the hush
of patient hangers. The chargecard.
The folded bathrobe
in the generous carrier.

*

Customer Services let me in, name
swinging on a clip-badge,
to the backstage of stairs and restless
swingdoors, through to
bulletin boards, focus groups, gossip.

Lunch; a few put-together tables;
now this writing game brings
people, persons, men and women,
their unwitting forays into a dream-life
electric when they read back:

which is when I love this work,
the written word like lucid dreaming
or the ritual of dance, the steps sure
and exploratory, their own meaning,
which anyone could paraphrase

but never get the measure of;
a German film crew filming everything
*just read that through again love*
to be dubbed for the gist of it,
what gets lost in translation.


\*


Downstairs, in the foodhall, not for the last time
I'm bewildered. Job done,
role put away, distraction gone
and everyone back at work.
There's this last thing, to walk in again,
as natural as I like, like the start of day
for the camera I mustn't look at.

There are items I might buy
and stand in that one person queue,
among 14 million each week
for tenderstem broccoli or tumbledry knitwear;
five items or fewer, tempted by
something sweet at the point-of-sale.

*for Chris Meade*

Smaller than its name and more human,
and more rigorous than its address.
The image drags it back in that sea
of undervalued poets it all but
foundered in and latterly resurfaced,
a surer arm at the helm, all hands on deck.
A rough, hefty democratic desk reminds me;
the possibilities round it too, bowed
by so much A4. I can't write ad-lib,
a friend in Doncaster said. Three years,
a hammock between 821
and 821.8; and to wake ten years later
still doing this is not to know
what to want, and get it.
A workshop for journalists to prove
they're poets too, and who may
write it up and sell poetry and some pens
that are themselves a sort of art. Mont Blanc.
There's coffee and the organisers
muck in, and for two hours
we go under for the beautiful stones
that once home will have dried dull. No,
for two hours we do writing games
and that is part of spreading the word
that could be theirs, yours, who knows, mine.

I'm an egg and chips bloke when I sit
to three bean soup; then downstairs for the BBC.
After, I kill an hour between trains,
my heart in my boots in Books Etc.
I know it's only a bad cold thinking aloud,
and that all of this
is a landlocked mountain
when all we ever need's the sea
and the illusion we can breathe water,
and to come back with our finds,
excited, 'Hey, look at this', and her or him
not 'So what?', but 'Yeah, I see what you mean.'
I know that.
Tell me something I don't know.

The most natural thing in the world
to sit crosslegged on a table in the canteen
and recite to the lunchbreak
for a wide-angled lens. But I listen instead
to a woman who says she is Fitted Tops, or Bodies,
and hear the pros and cons of alarm tags,
the teenagers who steal in bulk and steal to order.
Already the poem forms round the button
in the store detective's palm;
my daughter, thirteen, for a stunt as much as money,
five hours down the cop shop, prints taken
but let off with a caution. I don't mention this
or wonder where the new clothes come from
even now she claims aren't new. Released

to the shopping capital of the North,
at length down Grey Street for the Guildhall and quay.
I can buy a moonmap from Inner Space
or a *Big Issue* from the bloke outside.
Past Rothschild house, Milburn House. The Tyne
everything they say, only bigger, stiller, though stood there
it's me that's moving, upstream. Mild,
but even so there's an edge that pulls my scarf tighter.
Back uphill the day's heavy on my back,
money for old rope and what we use it for.
I can buy a 48 inch screen or a *Big Issue*
from the girl with the smile in front of it.

I'm met next to Crime in Waterstones by tonight,
two teachers who buy cake at four quid a slice,
then walk me to the University.
A twilight session with their MA,
to talk not poems but the small press,
more specifically how to get in print.
They note down facts and figures,
tricks of the trade and laugh like scripted.
Write what you are, I hear myself saying
only better than you are, more
vulnerable and confident, more true
and bugger being published. And if you can't
and even if you can, you have to get to know
the people in the know and sleep with them.

On the last train, a woman with her 9 year old
talks Glaswegian to me. She can't understand
a word I say. Three suitcases and a holdhall
by the guard's van, moving from a tenement
on the wrong side of some drugs guy
she spoke her mind to. To Scunthorpe,
a friend of her sister's. And if it doesn't work
in 6 months she'll go back and the council
will have to rehouse her. When the girl
goes to the loo, she tells me it was her,
her fingers in the till for a lad at school
that brought them here,
to meet a man at Doncaster she's not that struck on
with an Astra and a spare room for the kid,
life being what it is, not who you are.


ST MARY'S J&I, LONDON

M&S are big on community,
and Julia's weekly project is a school
five minutes from Baker St, which is why
I'm in a hall full of four year olds.
Out when I got round to phoning,
the teacher hasn't briefed me.
Half-hour sessions with combined classes
some of them multilingual
but not a word of English. April the first
and I wait for the punch-line.

Panic makes me calm.
I do rhymes: the one with the knickers and bra
works every time; though not,
I think, for Ali who hears only sounds
and the laughing like sharks.
The older groups write, computer
paper on the hard wood floor.
It works because they want it to
and when they read aloud the hall
like a church hall comes down to them,
snug and listening, the breath
between each small voice.

A boy reads and we see
the toggle that won't do
and mum getting back at last,
head in her hands, from work; a table,
his brother patting her shoulder, 'it's all right'.
Is this patronising? It's not fair
and anyone can see, however well
the teachers work it, the system's wrong.

*

*Poem: New Boy*

He picked a fight with himself and split his lip.
He poked himself in the back with a protractor.
He told tales on himself.
He threw his coat in the girls' toilets.
He made himself laugh in assembly
    and got called out to the front.
He knicked his maths book and wrote swearing all over it.
He knicked his ruler and wouldn't own up
    even though it had his initials on.
He flicked a rubber across the class and hit himself on the head.
He started bullying himself. No matter how early or late
    he was always there at the school gates.
He copied off himself. He got bad marks.
He kicked the back of his legs under the desk.
He forgot somebody else's PE kit.
He drank his own milk while he wasn't looking.
He called himself names. 'Hey four eyes'
    though he didn't wear glasses.

In D-Front foyer,
the mêlée of *Elle* and *Vogue, Women's Journal,*
journalists queuing to wander round with wine
the crush of talking-up next season.

That excitement, measured in turnover,
stays opaque, just clothes, without
the language to see cut and line,
the nuance that puts distance between

this chain and that. It's one woman shuttling
transatlantic with a slim case of decisions.
Meeting her, she seems too young, except
when she talks, kindly, friendly, shrewd.

You are what she says you wear, or else me,
dressed in Oxfam. She gestures with a glass
to the room, my notes, the olive-ochre of a jacket,
but it's not what she means.

Put it this way,
you have come to in a fridge
you have woken in a waiting room you've no memory of entering
you are shrinking on a train
day by day you are changing colour
you are invisible
you are orbiting the earth forever
whatever you say, however you say it, people laugh hysterically
you have bailed out at fifty thousand feet without a parachute
you are luminous
everyone assumes you are drunk
there's a cue ball in your mouth
you wake to find you're the opposite sex
you wake to find it's a decade later
you can talk only in rhyme.

## OVERHEARD ON A TRAIN

'Elaine, she says you won't remember her,
but you'll remember Olivia.
Australian, tall, in 87 or 88
in Market Harborough.
She says you bopped her, Olivia, twice.'

'Nope, can't place her.' (Boston, I look,
his voice Lowell's on the tape
pirated from the library:
sixty, jazz I guess or novelist.)

'Elaine. She says you'll know Olivia,
classy, backless dress, no tits.' The man leans back.
The jazz guy, or novelist, forward:
'Still nope. You say I bopped this woman.

Did I bop Elaine?'


## SHEFFIELD FAR GATE

The green plastic pallets of sliced white
wheeled through the food hall. The caged
fluorescence overhead. The price
of everything on stands or clipped to the edge.
The shelves themselves, stacked and faced
with pasta, marmalade, synthetic gold
of coffee dusty as you burst the foil:
the past rushing into its vacuum
with one remembering sniff at what it holds.

Walk through with a chargecard
to soft yards of wool and lambswool, shirts
and the largest market share of underwear.
This smile is you beside a pool,
swimwear that takes its lines
from lingerie. Brogues. The breathing racks
and knee-high mirrors to see
the shoes you're standing in. Lycra.
From design to bottled water;

from projected sales to the very last word
in gloves. Lighting and furnishings (mail-order),
from catalogue to juggernaut, from contractor
to the hydraulics in a loading bay,
the seasons are told in word and picture,
the weeks in tone and colour,
the days in weight and texture.

There's more, but what I remember's
the sliced, the caged, the stands and clips,
St Michael's Gold,
not the falling profits and falling shares
or the heads that rolled.


NORWICH

The man in store who organised it
is back from a ward where his father is dying.
Astonished to see us, there's no group.
Instead, the coat-tails of celebrity again:
a woman from the *New York Times*
with the article already blocked-out
in the canteen, the smoking room
although she doesn't actually herself.
I'm not thinking about this man's dad,
but mine, and money – her husband in telly,
her best-selling friend, her own first novel –
and about the word newsworthy.
I know about money, its usefulness,
the windfalls and sometimes
dead on my feet because I know no better.
200 miles and three hours to do it in
to teach tonight the finer points
of writing from the heart, for their MA –
a rung on a payscale or for love of it.
I talk poems and she scratches her arm
to check her watch while the diners mill past
like ghosts, though it's us who don't exist.

My father died at eighty five in a home
I visited just once. Its grounds were Byron's.
Madness, though he knew me for a moment.
A wheelchair for a man not big but never frail,
shyly full of himself and inclined
to childishness, everything only a bit of fun.
Pensioner by the time I could talk,
we never talked. I don't suppose he did.
Your father'll never be dead
while you're alive; but here I am, talking.
A room of nodding heads, a telly always on
and, beyond the tall Edwardian glass,
lawns lush as a golf course, the hurt call
of peacocks the place is famous for,
and banks of colour named into flowers.
Money can name anything,
and what it's called it is.
                                    On two floors or three
plastic changes hands for branded goods
whose quality's the company's good name.
You get what you pay for in this world,
especially if you're poor. Everything is worth,
as tradesmen say, what it will fetch.
Everything is words, Byron said,
and words were things to him,
and a small drop of ink, falling like dew
upon a thought, produced something new
that made thousands, perhaps millions, think.

You can say what you like to the dead
and when I didn't go again, no one
was surprised or asked me to, except me
and him maybe. I say, Do you have enough?
She shuts her book: More than,
and we part like friends outside the store
in 'Norwich, a drab East Anglian town …'
a piece, a friend will relish telling me,
that goes downhill from there,
while a man that moment for all I know
is talking to his dad, or not talking
for what it's worth, for all anyone can care.

# Apple

This one, you could halve it
with that penknife and wipe the blade
on your sleeve.
The pips go on forever.
A neighbour brought it with others from a tree

though it's
not to eat or put in a tart or crumble.
And not halved, or not yet,
though you can all but see
the flesh under the blade, almost feel
the pips on your tongue
before you spit them out, not cider

but the sour wine of doubt,
and you drunk all the same
on marriage, matrimony, wedded bliss,
or so you claim, and which you draw on
again and again, with no more idea
than the knife you hold here.
Well, my advice is, shut it
before somebody gets hurt.

## Pineapple

Where I come from they grow in tins
you see-saw open. The thrilling edge
to tempt a finger; the safe Carnation
on a swimming bowl. Sunday,
The Big Match or Big Film put away,
sliced white and tub butter to go with,
and History or Geog on dark nights
before the Palladium. But here
the world's shrunk to a shipping crate,
the striplight aisle of disposable income.
Look at these colours in black and white,
the grey of progress that brings prices down,
the beach to your kitchen. As I write,
the police search for someone in the air.
We hear and know the roters, the pressure
that keeps them up there. Also a deaf man
tells a sort of story on Three
in the code of a piano and his proxy.
It's not music but the thing itself:
two dimensions – a sketch of volume
and the space it sits in, the shades
of green and gold we bring to it – that bring
rings or chunks across the thirty years
between that Sunday tea and this. What it is
that grows on trees, what you pull the pin from,
so rich in vitamins A, B and C.

*Lemon*

The philosopher's blue one that proved
what anyone already knows, and the one
my daughter throws the way she would
the balloon she says it is. So new,
like polished or just-pulled from the dappled groves
of an impressionist last gasp,
and surprising in its weight and fall and lack
of bounce. The magnified-for-an-advert burst
of zest that twitches nostrils. Or the two we raced
from the corner shop down Slant Gate
one-in-four in a firework twilight.
What?
No, that's a person who unthinkingly joins a mass
movement, esp. towards headlong destruction.
Look it up. This is nothing like; is what you slice
or squeeze or grate the rind of or mistake
for half-deflated Christmas in April
with snow the size of money for hours
at the window but not settling enough
for a snowman. Who are you, anyway?
What are you doing here,
with your tart or snappy
disposition, more usually easily deluded
or taken advantage of, somebody in love
running several yards off the cartoon cliff
of taking a big messy bite expecting orange.

## Fruit Sestets and Coda

He was a small man, as if surprised peeling
a satsuma with his one hand. His desk
was huge and made of money. I sat this side
as directed, put my feet up as not, my task
to unwrap an orange, two being able
to play that game, the air pleasantly citrus

like goodbye or the people whose shadows played
across our faces in a foreign language.
I've come, spitting a pip, about the job.
A segment lay like Hebrew on his tongue. You've got
a nerve/no chance sunshine/a deal.
We raised our glasses. There was a waterfall

to walk to and a villa brilliant in the dusk,
so many windows to admire or put through.
My love, he said, do this one task
and later I did, in the starless lemon grove
drunk on being able to, the two of us
including him only by his absence.

By then it was too late, a peach orchard
or office that overlooks a lake at sunset;
and a plum in my mouth in the language
of commerce. And it was Judges 2, the verses
about disobedience and defeat
in which neither of us quite believe,

like living forever for a living
while night falls again as it must and the river
puts paid to its namesake by becoming a sea.

## Potatoes

The soil turns neatly as he brings them to light;
and me, bucketing them. That,
and the dog riding home on the barrow.
Next's a dusty paper sack my height
in the stone pantry, and Ted Savoury
planting it there from the dark
of his junk-shop van of fruit and veg.
And now those reds: the eyes, forgotten
till spring, bursting their pulpy skins
like the pipes in a poster of the heart.

Yes, I could wear his cap and jacket
despite the warm work: the tines, lifting,
would shake off what they came from.
But that's good for nothing but a spud gun
or halved to print a pattern to live down
or up to. If I'm digging, it's clearing
the back for a tree, like they say
you should for a new child.

# Chippie

Don't get me wrong. I believe in change.
Kebab it if you like, batter mars bars,
but this is my childhood, before pizza and tandooris,
the Balti Cottage next door to the Miner's Welfare.
This is formica counters too high, Tizer
and white tiles. Well yes, nostalgia's
not what it was, and it's the same for our lot,
in the lolling queue on Fridays
then back to unwrap them round the telly.
But sometimes you have to give in
to how it seemed to be, before vermicelli
and quick chill, before anybody'd died. A picture so real,
in three dimensions and sudden it stops you

like a glass door or seeing a friend
in the Open-All-Day three o'clock lull
and sidling next to him with 'Mek it twice, love,
he's paying.' – And of course he's been dead years.
And this bloke, startled, instead of anger
is trying to remember you, handing her
a tenner and grinning 'How you doing?'
(The sizzling splash of a bucket of raw chips.)
So you smile, too, you can't complain. Two grown men,
stood there while she shovels another portion
and lays another giant haddock on,
then steps back for both of you to lean
and season them at the same time.
'It must be ages,' he says. And you agree.

## To Autumn

You come breezing in. It's yours for a while,
make yourself at home. A leaf detaches itself
from how we look at it, dates are underlined
in still-to-be-backed books, and wasps
that helicoptered by dustbins are brown now

and taxi on the kitchen floor, their stings
the most alive thing about them. Danger, my dear,
come away. There are ash keys to show you
and conkers, fireworks to look forward to,
and Santa to believe in already in the shops.

## To John Keats from the Suffolk Coast
### for Dave and Annie Healey

Mr Keats to such as me, this side
of the water you crossed to be obsessed with,
but I'll call you John. You didn't care
for reverence, ordinary respect would do,
who might be with me or anyone,
at a dormer that looks on salt, unfinished water,
at night more stars and a half-moon brighter
than at home. I'm ten years older
than when you died, and two centuries
no further on; and not at that window
but sat up in bed in a cardie looking out
at November sun on a flat shifting surface,
smoking in a wooden house lent
on condition we understand it's a death trap.
Tongue and groove in a once fashionable grey;
a table loaded with shirts and cups, jewellery, books
and the hairdryer – before the car – we travelled
too light to bring. It's not for me
to tell you, which I can't do so well,
what you know or can't ever know, about
that thing no larger than an urn that explodes
and ravishes all silence, what is we've seeded
in the wide arable land of events. In my book
it's not even those Greek vases
impacted in one hologram of art
whose three dimensions spring when we read them
into living stillness. That is your genius.
I mean more than that, your gift for life,
the people, vulnerable, hacked to pieces
on their weakest side, that you saw whole
and loved enough to live in your thoughts
as surely as those swallows at dusk about the eaves
or that undrinkable claret raised to your lips,
whose bubbles colour and contain
this convex room, a stanza from your
posthumous existence. Those last months
a doctor's practised eye mistook arterial blood

(which you knew at once) and diagnosed the hurt
in your stomach that all the time
ate you inside out, and which lived on.
When they cut you open, your lungs
were all but gone, given to a final letter
that wanted for friendship's sake
to be remembered to your friends,
and adding 'I always made an awkward bow'.
Most of all I suppose I'm with that man
who, asked to choose someone from history,
would take you, John, to Waterstones
and show you the shelf-space that John Keats
occupies among the English poets, and why,
and – which no one could live to see –
who we are because of what you left,
what it is we are in what we make of you.

## Words for Paul Cézanne

The town museum banned me from its walls
till there wasn't a canvas it could afford.
By then I was fifty years dead, of course.
Not that I wanted for money or for the fame
that arrived late to drive me from home.
My friend Zola had his bestsellers and throve;
Renoir, whose one commission could buy
and sell me a thousand times, bought me.
I copied Chardin, Corbet; their fruit was flesh
just as it is, as if it might rot in the paint.
Mine was art. Don't look to me for life,
only oils and a palette knife. They say I walked
into Paris with my paintings on my back
like a Christ. A little joke, though it's true
you're tiny beside me and I'm humbled by it.
I loved my son. My wife was dutiful.
After, she said I'd no idea. I loved my home,
the landscape that grew out of me,
and you see how it answered. Not master
of myself then, or even in this,
I am a man who did not, does not exist.

*Moorland Landscape*
    *for David Blackburn* (Study for a Landscape Vision No.3)


Writing like this is writing from life
but seeing it new, a postcard of crushed-blue, blue
loved for itself in pastel
becoming snow.

Those lines that might be paths or drystone wall
suggest people among so much
snow or the idea of snow, breath that might
call a mirror to account,

a mirror 3-D with snow
in green, ultramarine, blue
on the edge of atonal, the brink
of melody, a canvas that seems lifesize
in a gallery and lifesize
on a card courtesy
Abacus (Colour Printers), Cumbria –

and which is in reality
an icelocked moor
propped on hot coffee to write from here:
a square mile and more of Yorkshire
which only might be Cumbria or/
and everywhere.

## On Dodd Fell
### for Ray Fisher


People seem meaningless
among so much abstract nature, the weather
that decides shades of green
in forests that fall to the valley like water
and among the huge wide moor.

Blobs of colour translate as gortex,
a tiny car running defines a road
and that road winds out the gradient
            to a small town:
and there to people, a meal, a joke invented
            over a pint, about Beethoven
so deaf he thought he was a painter.

Wensleydale. A friendly name,
its green-wax wheel of cheese local
but prized everywhere. Up here
it's a farmed wilderness that cuts art
            down to size,
the wind deafening and the gusts of rain
                                    easing off
to a late sonata of a landscape
eloquent
beyond words, like music.

# Top Withens

Moors that on this good walking day are hospitable in being empty far as the horizon, the cloud they merge in. Up here we might imagine like anyone three daughters set loose to be themselves and more than that in the opening out of lives peopled by characters, tiny seeds of a disease that flourished, biding its short time. Their mother dead before she knew them, their father had God to answer to, and answered. And so here we are, walking a wayward, invented, grey-green path guided by stories, bits of biography. The youngest is missing; disappointed, unremarked, thirty years old, she lies on a blue velveteen sofa in a cold room, admitting the doctor only in terror hours before she died. The middle girl also vanished. There's no point searching; there's only you. Even the eldest, who outlived them ten years to marry and wander here, bundled in words that broke her heart, recalling them and the brother they made not famous: it's no use. This little warmth of reconstruction, the thousands that pay the same homage, it can't hope to keep out the slight chill that killed her and the child she carried, however faithfully we remember what we think we know, or say out loud under a lightening sky her living name.

## Bus Station Café

There's a life here, the same mid-morning
for twenty or thirty of us, next to buses that pull in
to their stands at the plateglass, huge, out-of-scale.
The waitress tells the time by them,
and everyone who knows it remembers her name.

The menu is day-glo and home-made, grills mostly.
There's a chrome 24-hour face, and a fan
that like the slush-puppie never stops.
Pie-case ashtrays glint when the owner
goes round with a cloth collecting mugs.

The talk pauses while everyone looks
at a young woman, head on the table, drool;
concern, yes, but nobody's worried,
and sure enough she surfaces to seven frowns
becoming smiles, All right love? She's all right. We all are.

The local team has finally won something,
that programme was on again last night,
and listen to this, Jim's brother on the cruise ship,
he got a tip, not the sack like you'd think –
ten thousand dollars, that's six thousand quid.

Like this, this is a bloody cruise, the owner says,
pleased, wiping formica. In time the sun or moon
goes down a flight of steps to light a flooded cellar
where no one in dozens is wading to safety.
Which is to say, those of us with buses get them,

and the rest of us sooner or later leave anyway.

*Amsterdam*

His cock wandered off for the weekend,
came back to an empty house. (The heroes
who aren't dead are starting to die, not to mention
several relatives and even friends now, that sort of thing.
Also kids, kids had become an issue.) A week later,
the bread can walk by itself in the bread bin.

His boyfriend has left the planet, or so he's told,
which is where he remembers
the ancient history of Amsterdam
and the girl who made his cock wonder
if Mum wasn't right or his heart sometimes.
He lies down with crumbs and two packets
of Happy Shopper custard creams,

works the remote, makes black sweet tea,
dials 0898 but, her voice or his,
just can't concentrate. He doesn't cry
but if he did it'd be seeing that jumper
which by now can walk too, or his
(the boyfriend's I mean) shirt
crawling arm over arm to the washer.

# Chinese

China is a book he never wished to open.
Its villages and cities, rivers and mountains,
economy, history, art, there are others
who know about these. But here
in the middle of a week for middle management,
in the middle of a seminar, though he speaks
English, his English
listeners hear Chinese.
Something's wrong, he can see that,
understands what they're saying but not why.
He talks slower, louder. Their faces
are a picture of disbelief. One, with a tie
when everybody else's gone casual,
has a smattering and identifies it.
Cantonese. So our man says a few
simple sentences along the lines of
You're kidding me, and, Come on guys, this isn't funny.
But really no one's laughing. The dilemma
turns from him, discussed among themselves.
A breakdown, maybe, and him bilingual:
the stress, his own business
on the skids, why else would he be teaching us?
The one with the stammer thinks it's
all his fault, and in a way it is.
The man himself sits dumbfounded with
the hot sweet tea somebody's thought to make.
Is this permanent? Will he have to emigrate?

He tries writing, it's an ideogram.
When he mimes it's Noh Theatre.
Even his walk is a translation,

and the stars, when he has to get out
into the December dark, are unfamiliar
as his thoughts, a new mind-set
about the scheme of things, what it is
the wind means in the trees, and the rising moon,
and how horrible English tea is.
And so he walks with that walk like a dance,
cradling the cup still, up the lane, not going back
for his coat or
even looking back, leaving with no plan,
for no reason he could explain, or not to them.

# About Time

A ticking box, each second identical
as flakes that touch a roof and win a bet,
and as unique. Count them down with Big Ben
before you turn to kiss a stranger, let in luck
that is a slice of bread, a piece of coal, ten p.
Look back on moments as many, different
and the same, as people on the homeless streets
or redundant or in work that kills them, slowly,
or without family or with family they can't love.
Two thousand years and the church as full tonight
as superstores or *Songs of Praise*. The flakes
that fall and drift make most of us anonymous;
and though it's true that through them you can see
the changes – medicine, say – that no one would discount
what matters, it comes to me at last, is that the stranger
through the trackless snow has your name, mine.

*Twelfth Night or What You Will*


You're angry not because the tree's not down
and you're having to pack up Christmas on your own,
but because we're laughing in the kitchen
while the pizza hardens and goes brown.

Even the baby finds it hysterical,
planted in the middle of the table
she could crawl off, waving her wooden spoon
like a funny judge while we try and save the food.

The bright boa is round the mirror,
the filched holly taped up by the door –
when the lights are wound into their box
the New Year starts tonight, and what it lacks,

cold despite the fire, the radiators full on
despite the bills. In another town
a friend sets her face against cancer;
another's child died in the womb. Remember,

anyone could say as much, and a voice
might enter our heads, it's waiting for us.
Of course, even while we're playing Christmas,
Mary's first, our new life, our new house –

the bingo with mum on Boxing day,
like inviting Eric Cantona, as Katherine says,
for a kickabout, and that famous names game
where the boys chose the friends who came

because after all they're famous to us:
that's now and that's, for now, enough.
Talk sense. A voice like a cassette, as you walk
into a midnight wood. Let's let it talk

to itself for a while, and just step out
and see where this path leads and what we get
clearing out the superstitious debris
of a year whose debts anyone can see

are only money. We're in among
dense-dark trees which may one and one and one
displace the sense of a road the other side,
but the car's there even so, and, just serviced,

ten years old and four below, it starts first time,
to bring us to what we have, a home.
You feel it more than me, the others
in among the senseless endlessness of trees,

and if I take the world and you for granted, I'm sorry
that I don't just see it, that you have to tell me,
but you do *have* to tell me. I need your voice
so sometimes what we settle for is what we chose.

The salad's not burnt. The rest'll reheat
and the 'rather fine wine' will have time to breathe,
so we hoover round, laying the year to rest
in binbags in the cellar till the old year is the next,

keeping back the plastic santa and chewed card
that are toys now, and in under an hour
we pull up the sofa and eat, with a video in
and icecream for dessert, as if that's everything:

*Thelma and Louise*, it makes us feel good,
to make that wood, while we can, into a road
that's us, here, a film where enjoying it depends,
actually, on knowing how it ends.

## Teeth

The pain stops just being here, tipped back
like a space shot. One look and
'You don't like dentists,' he says. Fluent in gargle,
he understands my 'never met one'
is a joke that's true. Young, Asian, expert,
he drove up from the other end of a mobile number
on a Sunday in a black new Porsche
to calm me and put a bit of the wrong right.

A night and a morning kneeling by the sink
running cold across it brought me to this
partitioned room, the leather hydraulic chair,
besting thirty years of shame, as much as fear
and complacency, a weakness in character
that keeps my smile closed and lifts my hand
to a surprised laugh. And it's class and laziness too,
that gap between what's learned and what

you're born with. The heart is a muscle. Once,
to get a job, I lay in boxer shorts on a table
while a stethoscope gauged a murmur;
but denying advice is a habit second nature
as smoking or crunching sweets.
And so there's this. I submit to his white coat
and instruments, looking up into a sun
out of science fiction, while all the while

my wife holds my childish hand
just this side of fainting. It's over in minutes
and I can rinse and get unsteady to my feet,
white-faced in a drug company mirror.
'There's more to be done,' he says,
a man of understatement, and hands her his card
in case I change my mind
and who I am and want to be, from a family

with a grinning glass by the bed,
only wearing them for best, their faces wrong,
and slipping them in a hanky to eat.
What's left of mine's mine, and the damage too,
I know that. My talk's not one or the other,
theirs or ours in a world still us and them,
but one thing's for certain, I'll come back
only when it hurts enough.

## My Mother on a Seat Outside a Hospital

Too early for the bus, my mother
and her sister have walked a dozen dark-
to-daylight miles through a wood, by quiet roads,
to sit on a bench beside a flower bed,
colours that release their scent
in the evening, and to wait while her husband
dies on a ward already awake
that she might have visited after all.

He was the man before my father,
young, clean-shaven, just moved where work was.
If he'd not loved swimming so much
or had known that pool, which end was which,
or if he'd shallow-dived, I'd not exist;
and Mum too would be a different person,
spared the tragedy she mentioned
the other night in passing, a young wife
with two babies – my big sisters – and with my brother
forming inside her, who must manage
from that moment as best they can alone
in a strange town between the wars.

But there she is, just as she is, and so I can see
through that depth of water the spine
snapping, and the man who was not my father
bobbing to the air … It took him days to die
where, outside on a municipal bench,
two young women, girls they call themselves,
are anxious and not tired,
deciding to give it another half-hour –
despite the sixth sense that sent them there –
before bothering anyone so early.

## Soon

The King Street Methodist Mission
is gone. In three weeks of parking Tuesdays
in the Pay and Display (the Arts Centre that was)
it's come down from smart bombs – the plumbing hanging out –
to doll's house side, to a handful of rubble.
Wire netting and billboards fence an idea in
that some money-men had. And in a year
we'll barely remember the decades of livings
in paper shops, second-hands and chippies,
as if this under-one-roof complex, retail and leisure,
had always been here. And maybe it had.
For the moment the gap discloses a view
of the campus and Houses Hill. Sentimental
to want the past that's already changed
to insist it can't change. Change accelerates
quite sure it's right, and maybe it is.
Whatever values are freight on the canal
re-opened in the name of heritage,
it forgets the people eaten in the machinery,
the children in the endless dumbshow of looms,
the emphysema of a double-shift
that did away with daylight even on the longest days.
It's not all allotments and prize bands,
doors on the latch while the whole town goes
to the sea for a week.

                  And what was the Mission to me?
Once a year I might stroll past the wheelchairs
to browse upstairs, a library sale
of worn-out classics, encyclopaedias
ignorant of Aids and space flight, gazeteers
with half the world in pink, a world when books
were enough to get on and getting on was enough.
For such as us, it was. I see you now
with an orange box of knock-down titles;
for every one you bought, you said, you gave away
the same in shelf-space, those books you knew
you'd not re-read, and those you knew

you'd only ever meant to read. Stood here
this minute it astonishes me, after all this time,
to be astonished and still angry that you died.

## Death Cap
### for Pauline Bellamy

When the phone goes at ten past one
I'm already dressing, getting in the car,
the floored accelerator already
waking the whole street. But it's your friend

who was over this morning with a mushroom,
with the name of a mushroom I mean,
on the tip of her tongue all day,
saying it while she remembers. And so

the old woman sprawled where her heart stopped
between the loo and fallen walking frame,
the teenager with a wrist open to some despair,
the man who looked stupidly the wrong way

and stepped in front of what threw him in the air –
these, and the mugging, the rape,
the boy who choked to death on a boiled sweet,
they all belong to others, awake elsewhere.

And this, this mushroom, or its name,
is just a device to kill off not people
but characters, so many per chapter
like clockwork to the working out.

Leaves on the tree are thick night-lit green
at our window, making the room green
when I step back, though the searchlight
grazing our house isn't looking for us.

Being up and with nothing tomorrow
to be up for, we put the kettle on,
like people do
when there's nothing that anyone can do.

*Joiner*


Bread and jam to me, he says, burglary.
He slips our cheque in a loose back pocket
and promises an invoice for the insurance.
The window that eased off its hinges
will open now only to a dustbin through it,
the inner doors would need a pickaxe,
and the gardens front and back
light up like a football match at the slightest touch
of movement. Finally five lever chubb and bolts;
we've declined the alarm or shell
with realistic blinker at a fraction of the price.
Likewise the razorwire, moat and drawbridge
and the antimatter forcefield
he freewheels into round his sandwich:

and we laugh because it's funny
and it's funny because it's a joke
and if people stroll through sleeping people's homes
with a roll of binbags for the bits and bobs –
a camera, a jewellery box with a few quid of paste and sparkle,
the kids' first teeth and the sentimental value
of a baby's nameband – that's making a living
the only way some of us know how.

We laugh because it's timing,
the way he tells them, a natural talent
like running the country or Yorkshire Water,
but he's missed his vocation, the money
they make on the telly, astronomical …
A detour round the McCartneys' place,
Paulcatraz, returns him to his theme,
what you have to do to keep what's yours,

and why the poor take from the poorer –
not us (he has us down as teachers,
rich in this neighbourhood),
but we could join them and he could too,
just like that. He knows, he's been there,
which is why he shoulders
his last one-liner about the woman at 33,
and thanks us for the cuppa

and will see us again.

## Caveat Emptor

For twice this fair price
we might have bought a new one
with remote control and a guarantee.
But I don't have occasion to remark

on this wisdom yet, staggering happily
down her ginnel with it in my arms,
lowering it like a bomb or sleeping baby,
cushioned by my coat for the short ride home.

'We had it serviced,' she said, a grandma
in the spick and span of souvenirs
from other people's holidays, smiles
in dusted frames and all the cushions plumped.

We see thirty seconds of perfect working order,
'Couldn't sell it with anything wrong.' Oh but you could
to us, so much trust for such a little deal,
the way it shouts suddenly or blares

which the volume won't turn down. We don't
know it yet, and so I start the car,
the heater and radio on, the wipers now
through the brilliant giddiness of West Street

and on to the ring road, who never learn
about business and human nature,
back to the acreage of our Edwardian home
in a slum with its umpteen radiators

and bills through the roof. And though
we've swapped the family credit
for more niggly evidence
to plug in and stretch out infront of,

our baby and the kids prove otherwise,
which is just as well being how we are,
putting it down to luck that any moment
surely has to change, as if just thinking that

could make it change,
which it can of course and will.

## You'll Like This

Word of mouth from dinner packs the evening out,
and what he learned then he puts in now:
names, mainly, for butts of jokes and flattery
like clairvoyance. Best is completely at random
to bring the local hardman up on stage
blind in the lights, polite. And to lift a tenner,
and to open his mouth by turning an ear
for an egg to pop out and calling him duck.
Pit villages, he has all the patter, near the knuckle
on inbreeding and the little lad lost in the wood,
but he's a highwire act and risk is part of the trick.
Committee men's nicknames put him good
and 'Society Row' at Edlington.
It's a night out alright and they split their sides
while he's straightfaced through the wreckage,
a little man still rough round the edges,
wide-eyed, brilliant, desperate, two years from telly …
When the hardman twigs and goes to go for him
but can't get off the stool. The air's blue
with what he'll do to him and to this lot,
the men he's shat on, women he's been through,
all of them crying with laughing,
till a click of the fingers releases him,
the last half hour blank and the conviction
that that onion's a granny smith. Finally,
handing him grandly from thin air a tenner
for being a sport, with the understanding
he'll stand some of these many good friends a drink.

## Hayfever

Dust mask and wraparound shades
or fishbowl helmet with a hoover tube to filtered air;
twice the dose of a proprietary brand
sending your heart haywire;
sitting in a cellar or rowing out to sea:

your face still comes up
like a mismatch in the ring and you sneeze
without pause, your eyes heartbreak
or a broken tap. Venturing out to the cool
of a supermarket is humiliating
but you're not at death's door. Let's get this

in perspective. It's only an allergy,
and however you shower them
nobody'll catch it. Nothing's going off
in your blood: cut here
and anyone can drink it quite safely
or a pint, if they like, of your saliva.

Such a lovely name, winding lanes,
golden oceans to wade through, this cousin
to asthma and eczema, the merest trace
of peanut that killed an athlete this morning.
And gone by the end of Wimbledon,
forgotten at once like the hiccups till next year

surprises you with a lungful
of your body saying no, your eyes and nose
on red alert, a kneejerk prejudice
that brings you to your knees
forcing harmless motes out
at nigh nigh nine-
ty miles an hour repeatedly.

## Pediculus Humanus

i
We lather it on each other's heads
and reminisce about the week in the Lakes
we came back with scabies. 90°
everywhere but Cumbria, where it rained.
The best holiday we've ever had. And what's this

to that? An epidemic,
the first chemist said, stepping back
to lift a little bottle from the empty shelf.
But we're a tribe at holiday time
and though lice, the leaflet says, can't jump
they can certainly crawl. We can't get by
if we don't put our heads together
and at night, on the one pillow,
what nit's to know whose head is whose?

ii
Weeks later and sixty quid lighter,
and they're still there, breeding at a rate
you'd need a calculator. More days
of tea-tree oil and finetooth combing:
and there's another in the youngest's parting,
untouchable, in Produce in Sainsbury's.

iii
There's always vinegar, I remember.
My head over the huge Belfast sink
and my big brother, *the buggers don't like this.*
And they didn't, but I bet they do now.
Picture them lazing in it, butterfly, breaststroke,
guzzling it down, sending out for pizza
until we really look. Alien, mediaeval,
all hooks and claws through a lens
in the pool of an anglepoise, jagged
as a fjord, armoured plump red
and very much alive
with something of you, something of me.

iv
Their poisons are contamination, what we say
when we feel lousy. It was fleas,
not rats, that brought the plague, and these
cut down to size with a playground name,
some pettiness over minor detail.

And they won't be killed, pickaxe in
to the scalp and hang on, cement their eggs
as a metaphor, their next generation
already immune to what did for them:
me and you, us and ours, their hosts.

v
Listen, the up-close outsize itching in the dark,
that's them, feeding. We'd almost rather be bald.
If we all at the same time
shaved like swimmers, or Sigourney Weaver …

And then I see our Olga,
in that wig that cost Tom a packet,
and who was beautiful anyway,
him being so close – from her illness – to losing her.

I can't remember ever combing your hair.
Let me comb your hair.

## Beard

At twenty, needing to look older
than fourteen, I grew one that lived with me
ten years. Clipped trim, and with that hair –
though I didn't admire him – people said
'Noel Edmunds.' 'Well, if I had his millions …'
Still expecting I would. Not that full-face black,
mountaineer or deputy head, looking down
from the clouds; nor the raggedy don't-mind-me,
men who, even built like prop row forwards,
manage to look small. I know, I know lovely,
wiser, brighter men than me carry one off,
even a goatee, and wasn't it Thatcher
who wouldn't have a beard in the cabinet?
Two sides to every stereotype, but mine
was a boy's, and my wife finally told me
to grow up. I thought of this knicking the tip
of my nose with a fixed head disposable.
There's time to grow whiskers, Dad said,
when you're six foot down. He was wrong.
And they'll burn me too, wet shaved
to just the same blush, though what I remember
or say I do is the bits of loo roll
that gave way in the end to silvery stubble
like a hermit or a sage, the mask he wore
when nothing made sense, alone there
in that place among so many of his kind.

*Story*

I'm hearing this. A river, constant,
full of itself in the river,
people down in the kitchen, chewing over
some remarkable event, a little scandal
that flared at the edge of their own lives.
They see back a week, a month into it.
The words aren't clear, but a name
reaches me, a friend of a friend. I see them
by the clink of a plate, a breakfast cup,
predicting how things will change

because of this juicy, out-of-character
waywardness. Their who'd-have-thought-it faces
are humanly alive with gossip.
I know the story, the man
who fell for another man, what he learned
one night about himself. I know his family.
I look out across the valley
turned pink by a new day, and think of him,
that new person, the one
he was meant to be or to incorporate,
and the death that knocked me sideways,
and then remember the baby, real
as my breath in this cold guest room.

Him, my age, similar sort of looks,
with the same scruffy taste in jeans and jumpers
and elegant women, my wife and his.
If we'd been different, and friends,
we might have congratulated ourselves,
how did we manage that, being only us
and loved for only being us,
whatever that is, whatever anyone might say.

## Self Portrait with Lightbulb

and stepladder, of course, it being the one
on the landing that took a half-drop of wallpaper
and has a too-short flex. Enclosed three-sides round
by a pink darker than it looked in the shop,
it'll stay gloomy here where the shade
won't admit a higher wattage. The ladder's splashed
with mostly white emulsion and the treads,
you can just see, are grooved, non-slip. But not,
as is painfully obvious, entirely safe.
That space-walk posture
is free-fall where I'm about to fall, backwards
into the well of the stairs, the thirty feet
of letting go just wide enough where the turn
of the banister will allow my flailing grasp
to pass unhindered. But here
I'm stopped, idiotic, hair like a gale,
and the side of my face comically astonished
though quite secure in that closed-shutter
instant of thin air, the bayonet bulb
still in hand and held out as if I thought
it was lit up like a new, quite brilliant idea.

# Wye

Yesterday we drove from a festival
heavier with books we don't need and more crockery
and with the ring you lost
(that didn't this time turn up in a glove)
replaced by an amber stone in silver,
from a street stall dearer than the first gold.

It was work but like
a second honeymoon, a weekend by the Wye
without the kids for once.
A moonless walk beside the river to a table
they forgot to set, and the girl,
reminded of our still-empty glasses,
'Another bottle of the same?'

I was a waitress just like her,
you say surprising me
with another of those pre-us selves,
forgetting, muddling, upsetting soup
into a lap, twice in fact, the same polite man,
and getting the best tips.
For a while you're this girl, sixteen,
just finished in the small hours
walking a mile across a frosty town
to a flat with french windows and a goldfish.

OK. But that ring,
think what it cost before you lose it,
then lose it if you like, it's yours.